festivals

around the world

Godfrey Hall

Wayland

Titles in this series:
Clothes Around the World
Festivals Around the World
Food Around the World
Houses Around the World
Musical Instruments Around the World
Shops and Markets Around the World
Toys and Games Around the World
Transport Around the World

Cover pictures: A dancer at the Rio Carnival in Brazil. Models at the Independence Day celebrations in Delhi, India. A float at the Gion festival, Japan. Children dressed up for 'Trick or Treat', Baffin Island, Canada.
Contents page: Children celebrating Holi.

Book editor: Alison Cooper
Series editor: Deb Elliott
Book design: Malcolm Walker
Cover design: Simon Balley

First published in 1995 by
Wayland (Publishers) Limited
61 Western Road, Hove
East Sussex BN3 1JD

© Copyright 1995 Wayland (Publishers) Limited

British Library Cataloguing in Publication Data
Hall, Godfrey
    Festivals Around the World. – (Around the World Series)
    I. Title II. Series
    394.2

ISBN 0 7502 1564 X

Typeset by Kudos Design Services
Printed and bound by Rotolito Lombarda S.p.A., Italy

Acknowledgements
The publishers would like to thank the following for allowing their photographs to be reproduced in this book: Bryan and Cherry Alexander *cover* (bottom right), 22; Chapel Studios 14 (Tim Garrod); Eye Ubiquitous *cover* (bottom left) and 9 (Frank Leather), 12 (James Davis Travel Photography), 13 (Helen Lisher), 16 (James Davis Travel Photography), 19 (top, James Davis Travel Photography), 21 (bottom, David Cumming), 24 (James Davis Travel Photography); Chris Fairclough 8 (top); Sally and Richard Greenhill 8 (bottom); Robert Harding 11 (Adina Tovy), 19 (bottom), 27; Hutchison Library 5 (top, Sarah Murray); Impact *cover* (top right, Ben Edwards), *contents page*, 6, 7 (Mark Cator), 10 (Ken Graham), 17 (David Gallant), 25 (bottom, Gavin Milverton), 28 (Christophe Bluntzer); Panos 15 (top, Marcus Rose), 25 (top, Penny Tweedie); South Somerset District Council 26; Tony Stone Images *cover* (top left, Donald Nausbaum), 4 (Ulli Seer), 5 (bottom, Ed Pritchard), 15 (bottom, Glen Allison), 18 (David Baird), 20, 23, 29 (Rohan); Zefa 21 (top).

Contents

Festival fun

At festivals, people celebrate things that have happened in the past and look forward to the future.

At many festivals, people like to dance and listen to music. These musicians are playing at a festival in Germany.

Sometimes people dress up in beautiful costumes and take part in a parade.

All over the world, people enjoy watching firework displays at festivals.

Religious festivals

Many festivals celebrate important events in different religions around the world.

Hindus celebrate the festival of Holi in spring. They throw coloured powder over each other and play tricks. Special food is eaten and bonfires are lit.

Easter is also a spring festival. Christians remember the death of Jesus and celebrate his rising from the dead. Many Christians gather in Jerusalem, where they believe the events of the Easter story took place.

More religious festivals

The Jewish festival of Hanukah takes place in December. This girl is lighting the Hanukah lamp.

During the holy month of Ramadan, Muslims do not eat between sunrise and sunset. At the end of Ramadan, they have a festival called Eid ul-Fitr, where special food is eaten. People also give each other presents.

Gion is an important festival in Japan.
Huge floats like this one are pulled through the
streets. People sit in the floats playing music and
waving fans.

Seasonal festivals

Some festivals are held to celebrate the changing seasons.

In Alaska, people make the most of the snowy winter. They make giant sculptures out of ice.

Winters in Sweden and Finland are cold and dark, but in the summer the days are very long. At Midsummer, people celebrate the long days with music and dancing.

Flower festivals

In The Netherlands, people hold processions to celebrate the growth of beautiful tulips and daffodils. They use the flowers to decorate floats.

Flowers are important in the Channel Islands too. On one of the islands, Jersey, they have a festival called the Battle of Flowers. They make giant models out of flowers.

Food festivals

This is a harvest festival in Japan. At a harvest festival, people give thanks for the crops that have grown.

These musicians are playing at a fishing festival in Nigeria. They are celebrating a good catch of fish.

Every autumn, there are wine and beer festivals in towns and villages along the River Rhine in Germany. People celebrate the harvest and enjoy music and dancing.

Animal festivals

In Switzerland and Austria, the cattle are brought down from the mountains at the end of the summer, to graze in the lower fields. The cattle are decorated with flowers and led through the village streets.

In some countries, there are special religious services for animals. People bring their pets, and even farm animals, to be blessed by a priest.

Water festivals

Many festivals take place on a river or sea. In Hong Kong, the Dragon Boat races take place in the harbour. There is a dragon's head on the front of each boat.

People enjoy watching the yachts at regattas like this. The big sails of yachts fill with wind as they race along.

In Thailand, there are boat races and parades along the river during the New Year festival. The festival is called Songkran.

Carnivals

Carnivals take place all around the world. There are parades with singing and dancing. People dress up in colourful costumes. The most famous carnival takes place in Rio de Janeiro in Brazil.

This is the Mardi Gras carnival in New Orleans, in the USA.

In August, there is a big carnival in Notting Hill in London. This girl is taking part in the parade. She is wearing a spectacular red costume.

Children's festivals

In the USA and Canada, children like to play 'Trick or Treat' on October 31st. If the people they visit do not give them a treat, the children play a trick on them.

In Japan, they celebrate Girls' Day and Boys' Day.
On Girls' Day, special dolls are put on display in
the girls' homes. Some of the dolls are very old.
On Boys' Day, each boy flies a streamer in the
shape of a carp. The carp is a river fish that is said
to be very brave as it swims up the river.

Remembering the past

People in the USA celebrate the Fourth of July. On that day, about two hundred years ago, the American people decided they were going to rule themselves, instead of being ruled by Britain.

The Australians celebrate Australia Day on 26th January. This was the day, just over two hundred years ago, when the first British people came to live in the country.

In Britain, November 5th is Guy Fawkes' Night. There are bonfires, processions and firework displays. Almost four hundred years ago, Guy Fawkes tried to blow up the Houses of Parliament and kill the king.

Local festivals

Some festivals take place in only one town or village, or in a small area of a country.

Punkie Night in October is very special for the people of Hinton St George in Britain. The children parade through the streets with lanterns and sing the Punkie Night Song.

In some villages in Derbyshire, in Britain, people 'dress' the village wells with pictures made out of flowers. They have done this every year for hundreds of years, to show that they are glad to have enough clean water to drink.

City festivals

Every year a new Lord Mayor of London is chosen. The Lord Mayor travels through the city in a grand procession. You can see him waving from the golden coach.

Chinese people live in cities all around the world. The Chinese New Year is a very important festival for them. There are noisy parades and dragon dances in the areas where most Chinese people live.

Glossary

beer   An alcoholic drink.

costumes   A costume is a set of clothes. It is usually different from the sort of clothes people wear every day.

crops   Fruit, vegetables and grain that are grown for people to eat.

floats   Decorated carts or lorries without roofs. They are used to carry people and models in a procession.

graze   Eat grass.

harvest   Gathering in fruit, vegetables and grain when they are ready to eat.

lanterns   Lights that can be carried. They were used a lot in the past before torches were invented. Now they are usually only used in parades at festivals.

parades   Groups of people marching or walking together, or travelling on floats. Often there is a band playing music too.

regattas   Races for sailing boats or rowing boats.

sculptures   Models.

wells   Places where water bubbles up out of the ground, or deep holes that are dug to reach water under the ground.

yachts   A yacht is a kind of boat.

Books to read

Celebrating Festivals Around the World by Capel
   (Temple Lodge Press, 1991)
Let's Celebrate series (*Spring, Summer, Autumn, Winter*) by Rhoda
   Nottridge (Wayland Publishers Ltd, 1994)

More information

Would you like to know more about the people and places you have seen in the photographs in this book? If so, read on.

pages 4–5
A band at a beer festival in Munich, Germany, wearing traditional dress.
A girl in a colourful costume at the Notting Hill carnival, London.
Fireworks have been used for thousands of years, in celebrations all over the world.

pages 6–7
Holi takes place in February or March. It is an especially important festival in the country areas of northern India, where the powder-throwing sometimes gets out of hand!
Christians following the Way of the Cross in Jerusalem.

pages 8–9
Hanukah is the Jewish Festival of Light. A candle is lit on the first day of the festival. An extra one is lit each day, until all eight are burning together.
Eid ul-Fitr is celebrated when the new moon marks the end of Ramadan. Muslim families try to be together for this important festival.
Gion is a festival of the Shinto faith. The festival began in Kyoto, the former capital of Japan. Shintoism is the main Japanese religion.

pages 10–11
The ice sculptures are created at the Fur Rendezvous in Anchorage, Alaska.
People are dancing round the leaf-covered pole. This is similar to the British tradition of dancing around a 'maypole' threaded with bright ribbons.

pages 12–13
Flower parade in Haarlem, The Netherlands.
The Battle of Flowers started in 1902, when a flower festival was held to celebrate the coronation of King Edward VII. After the festival, people armed themselves with flowers from the decorations and the Battle began.

pages 14–15
This Shinto shrine is in Tokyo, Japan.
This fishing festival is held at Argungu in Nigeria.
The women at this Munich beer festival are wearing traditional dress.

pages 16–17
Cattle being driven down through Kitzbuhel in the Austrian Tyrol, to the lower pastures where the grazing is better.
This service of blessing for animals is taking place in Suffolk, Britain.

pages 18–19
The Dragon Boat races are held in May or June. The Dragon Boat festival marks the death by drowning of a famous Chinese poet over two thousand years ago.
The Cowes Regatta. Cowes is a town on the Isle of Wight, an island just off the southern coast of Britain.
The Thai New Year is in April. Buddhism is the main religion in Thailand and statues of the Buddha are carried in the processions.

pages 20–21
Many carnivals are held in February or March to celebrate Mardi Gras. 'Mardi Gras' is a French expression which literally means 'Fat Tuesday'. The Mardi Gras celebrations in Rio and in New Orleans are particularly famous.
The Notting Hill carnival was started by the West Indian community in that area of London.

pages 22–3
'Trick or treat' is especially popular in North America. It takes place on the same night as Hallowe'en.
Girls' Day takes place on March 3rd and is also known as the Dolls' Festival. Boys' Day is on May 5th. Models of samurai armour and helmets are sometimes displayed in the boys' homes.

pages 24–5
This Fourth of July parade is taking place in New Orleans, Louisiana, USA.
The first British settlers landed in Australia on January 26th, 1788. This firework display is taking place over Sydney.
The Gunpowder Plot to blow up King James I took place in 1605 – Guy Fawkes was just one of the plotters. The town of Lewes in East Sussex, Britain, is famous for its Guy Fawkes celebration. People parade through the town bearing flaming torches.

pages 26–7
Hinton St George is in Somerset, Britain.
Well dressings traditionally show scenes from the Bible: this one shows Noah's Ark.

pages 28–29
The Lord Mayor's Show takes place in November each year.
The dragon or lion used in the dances at Chinese New Year is supposed to scare away evil spirits and bring good luck.

Index